Hackensack Regional Chamber of Commerce

How to Make Your Membership Give You the Most Return on Your Investment

How to Make Your Membership Give You the Most Return on Your Investment

By Hackensack Regional Chamber of Commerce

situation. This work is sold with the understanding that the Publisher is not engaged in rendering legal, accounting, or other professional services. If professional assistance is required, the services of a competent professional person should be sought. Neither the Publisher nor the Author shall be liable for damages arising here from. The fact that an organization or Web site is referred to in this work as a citation and/or a potential source of further information does not mean that the Author or the Publisher endorses the information the organization or Web site may provide or recommendations made. Further, readers should be aware that internet Web sites listed in this work may have changed or disappeared between when this work was written and when it is read.

Executive Director: **Darlene Damstrom**

Edited/Proofed by: **Betty Shingelo and Lillian Freitas**

Special Assistance by: **Donald Perlman**

Cover Design by: **Usama Waqar**

Interior Design by: **Usama Waqar**

Copywriting/Production: **WILD Wendy Richmond**

IMPORTANT NOTE FROM HACKENSACK REGIONAL CHAMBER OF COMMERCE

This book is not intended to be either legal or ethical advice. Our goal is for this book to inspire you. Just know that whatever strategy you use to grow your business, you should know why things work or don't work, so you don't end up needlessly losing your investment in joining our membership.

Any copies or advertising used in this book are not to be used exactly as written. They are for educational and instructional purposes only.

Neither the author nor the publisher makes any warranties, either express or implied, about whether any of the enclosed documents, materials or instructions are legally or ethically appropriate for your business. Neither the author nor the publisher accepts any responsibility or liability whatsoever for the legal or ethical appropriateness of any of the enclosed marketing documents, materials or instructions and/or your use of the same. If in doubt about the appropriateness of legality of any materials or instructions, you should obtain proper guidance.

No income representations are made. Some business owners learn the material in this book, take massive action and reap the financial, emotional and lifestyle benefits that follow. Others will read this book, believe they have now "done the work" on their membership investment but won't follow through with anything else. Whether or not you make money with this book depends on taking action, and the type of product or service you offer.

SPECIAL THANKS

We, at the Hackensack Regional Chamber of Commerce, would like to thank the Chamber Members for making our Chamber so successful. Also, we would like to thank the Board of Directors for seeing this book as a great asset for our current as well as potential members.

We thank the HRCC Membership Committee for assisting in putting this book together and a special thanks go to WILD Wendy Richmond for bringing her inspiration, talent and service to making this book happen.

TABLE OF CONTENTS

PREFACE

Why We Wrote This Book

1. **As a "thank you" to our current members:** We know how challenging it is in today's business world with all of the competition for all businesses. Because of this, we wanted to create a resource that our current members could use to help grow their businesses and get back much more than what they invested to be a part of our membership.

2. **To show you proven strategies you may not have thought about to utilize your membership:** Through the various examples written in this book, you will be able to see other examples of how successful Chamber members are utilizing their membership to achieve their goals. If you read this book, look for strategies you are not currently implementing. You may find many more possibilities for achieving and exceeding your goals for joining.

3. **To break "Myths" about membership:** Part of this book is about breaking myths about joining the Chamber. You will read examples of successful Chamber members who do things that other unsuccessful Chamber members are not doing or will not do. Please see that success leaves clues. If you read and observe, you will find hidden and not so hidden success strategies that can multiply your

return on investment in becoming a Chamber member.

4. **To make it easy to be a member:** Even in these challenging times, there are easy ways to make your Chamber membership work for you and your business. You will read about them in the following chapters as well as in the *Special Success Strategies* chapters at the end of this book.

We hope you enjoy reading this book and come away with a renewed sense that you can get everything that you want from the Chamber and, we bet, even more than you ever imagined!

MEET SUCCESSFUL CHAMBER MEMBERS

Since there are many different approaches to being a successful Chamber member, we wanted you to see and read other success stories. If you keep your mind open to others' ideas, you may find some great things that you have never thought before.

Every business that comes into the Chamber has a different reason and goal for joining. In this book, you will read about various ways you can make your membership with the Hackensack Regional Chamber of Commerce give you back a maximum return.

Disclaimer: ONLY IF YOU READ and TAKE ACTION!

CHAPTER One

Darlene Damstrom
Executive Director

Hackensack Regional Chamber of Commerce

I have been the Executive Director of the Hackensack Regional Chamber since April 2001. This puts me in my 14th year. I did not have a business of my own. I came in through, Anthony Ursillo, who has been an active member.

What I like most about being the Executive Director is that I'm able to bring members together and have them forge relationships to do business with one another.

We have a member who is quite active and is the Chairwoman of our Education Committee. When Stacey first came to us her business was only an idea. This goes to show how you go from start up to success.

Our office is also a resource center with SCORE. We have retired business executives that come in and assist local potential business owners in starting a business. Stacey came to my office to utilize those services. I had a counselor from SCORE meet with her regularly and the two of us got to know Stacey. In trying to help her a name for her business was born, "At Home

Companions." It is a Home Health Aide business.

From that point, Stacey was seeking some space to do a training class and was also seeking potential health aides for her business. We offered her the use of the Chamber office to do that as well.

It's very nice to see how somebody starts from the bottom and becomes successful. Stacey wound up with a very successful business, successful enough that she's dedicated herself to our Chamber.

At the table, Stacey asked Kevin Vernieri, another person who sits on the committee who sells long term health care, about policies and now they do business with one another. It comes full circle and now Stacey does business with other members. She reaps the benefits of the Chamber and as Co-Chair of the Education Committee, gives back to the community via scholarships.

Recommendations to Get Your Investment in the Chamber Back After You Join

I think new members have to come in with the mindset that they have to participate. I hear a lot of stories as we go down the road from salespeople, in particular, that say "Well I haven't gotten any business." I question how often do you attend an event? Have you reached out to other members? We provide an Excel spreadsheet of all our members which allows them to make their own introductions.

We don't say solicit but perhaps: "I'm a fellow member who surely would love to meet with you. Maybe we'll do lunch. Maybe we'll meet at the next networking event". If you don't experience some of our events or events that we bring forward from other Chambers through a consortium, then I think you're not working as hard as you can to get to where you need to be.

We can only bring you the resources and it's really up to you to get involved. If joining a committee is not for you and you like only after-hour events, we have a myriad of opportunities. There are events that take place morning, noon and night that you can attend and meet some of these potential customers. It is your responsibility to put in the work. It's not going to come to you. We can't bring everybody to you. We can only make the introductions. We can definitely put you in touch with businesses that are in the same field as yours and that feed from the same clientele. You can work together. We see a lot of that happening also.

Great example of getting like businesses together

I receive many calls from people inquiring about any commercial property available. Is there anybody that I could recommend?

Here's a good example of getting businesses together. We had somebody coming from Long Island looking to purchase or lease property in Hackensack. They needed a commercial broker as they were in the insurance business; and because it's centralized, they have certain criteria they must follow. I put this company in touch with one of our commercial brokers and from there they found a property, built the establishment and that business became a Chamber member.

"It all kind of works together"

One member recommends the other and it all comes together if they can work collectively. That's really the point; you have to be able to work together. We could have members in the publicity and marketing field but we might have businesses that utilize these services outside of our Chamber members. If only our Chamber members in those businesses would introduce themselves and work together. If **it's not today**, it could be six or nine months but they will remember you.

That's the whole thing, making them remember you; or if they know somebody who needs that service they might make a recommendation. *"Wow, I met this really great guy, really great gal, at this networking event through this Chamber, give them a holler."* That's how these things are done.

"Become Part of Your Local Community"

In many cases, there is a community member in need. Our members have rallied together, donated their time and their services to help someone. Whether its a donation of a rental truck to help a family move furniture or turkeys for Thanksgiving our members always step up to help.

I am always amazed at how our businesses will work together, at no monetary advantage, to make sure their community has what it needs. A few years ago, our membership decided to hold an event specifically to raise money for scholarships for local high school students. That program is now developing further to help employees of member businesses to better themselves.

"You Get Back What You Give"

Some people don't understand what a Chamber could do for them. Does it work for everybody? Not any one business or organization could work for everybody. If you give it all you have we'll match that and we'll try to make all the magic happen. The Chamber has the needs of each member business in mind. Each member who is successful makes the Chamber that much stronger.

We have great businesses and we've got great members. It's just a matter of getting everybody together. Sometimes it's very hard because what interests one may not interest the other.

Why Join & Participate?

The best thing about our Chamber is that we happen to have one of the friendliest Boards of Directors that you will ever come across.

At times, we have over 20 individuals sitting on our Board that never leave the table unhappy. They are always working with one another to make the best decisions for their members; and that's important. You need somebody that you could rely on, that you trust and that you built a good relationship with.

Our friendly Board and members are the best feature of our Chamber. We'll get the work done. **We'll work hard with you**, but remember: **"with you" not "for you"**. We are very friendly and we will do everything we can as a Board and committee to help you make it happen.

You can find Darlene at: info@hackensackchamber.org or www.hackensackchamber.org.

CHAPTER  TWO

Dr. Richard Santucci

Chiropractor, Bergen Family Chiropractic Center

My name is Dr. Richard Santucci. I've been a chiropractor in Hackensack since 1977. As the name states, we are Bergen Family Chiropractic Center. We take care of everyone from newborns to 99-year-olds-plus. We just keep humming along and the basic thing we do is to try to keep people as healthy as we can.

I have been a member of the Hackensack Regional Chamber of Commerce at least 10 or 15 years. My wife is a former president. What I like most about being a member of this Chamber is that I've always been a very social person with a lot of contacts so I am sort of the "Go To" guy. People will call me up and ask me for recommendations for anything from a plumber, to an electrician, or a maintenance person and I always have somebody reputable for them.

The Chamber was another natural outreach for me to **meet even more good people that I could refer.** When the need arises and someone says *"I need an auto body guy,"* I tell you to call *"this" guy*. You need somebody here, you call that guy, whatever it may be. At least these are people who I know and socialize with. **It expands your network of not only business contacts but friends.**

I became a member because of my wife's involvement. I was a member years ago but I let it lapse because the Chamber wasn't very active. Since then, the Chamber has made a major turnaround for the better and now it's phenomenal. It's one of the best Chambers out there. It's really active. It's very visible and it's beneficial to become a member.

What Changed in the Hackensack Regional Chamber of Commerce?

They have a lot more events, meet and greets, additional marketing events, meet your neighbors and your fellow business people, etc. They do many good things like that to promulgate visibility within the community.

A success story ...

There's been so many little things. Somebody will call me up and say "I have a worker who got hurt. Can you help them?" We will certainly take care of them.

We have one little child who came in with a developmental disability. He was about three and was unable to walk. His parents had to hold him and take him to all kinds of pediatric neurologists. We put him on a program of adjustments and changed a couple of things in his diet. Now he's a happy little boy. He is no longer going to the pediatric neurologist. He is walking on his own. He's about six years old now and has come a very long way. Now he runs into the office, which is very satisfying.

This referral came through the Chamber and as far we are concerned, being able to help this young child made our day.

You refer out other members of the Chamber

I refer out other members of the Chamber all the time. Whenever it's appropriate, I go through the Chamber list. Most of these people you know off the top of your head. Because you know them, you do business with them; sometimes you even have dinner with them.

Recommendations for getting more from the Chamber

I would say to keep a little book like a telephone book, but don't put the name of the business down first because you may not remember it. If it's plumber, you list it under "plumber" and use the business name. If it's an electrician, you list it under "electrician" and you put the business name and the contacts. This way when someone inquires about needing a good plumber, you know who to call. You look them up because you may not remember George's name. You don't use him all that much but you know he's there. You know he's a member and you know he's reputable. It's just an easy reverse directory for you because you're cataloging it under the service as opposed to the business name.

Join the Chamber, it's a good opportunity to become a referral source

It's like other business networks, International BNI or LeTip or any of those, joining the Rotary or Lion's Club. It's **the repetitiveness of meeting people** and asking how's this, how's that, how's your kids, whatever it may be. You have to establish a relationship with somebody before you can get to the point of building trust; before you get to the other point, which is doing business. If you don't establish the bottom of the triangle as a relationship you're not going to get up to the point, which in this case is earning trust.

They've got to know I can call that guy and get an honest answer. He'll give me the best deal. He'll do whatever it is he's supposed to do to facilitate solving my issue.

You can find Dr. Santucci at: www.bergenfamilychiro.com

CHAPTER Three

Meryl Surgan

Supplemental Insurance Expert and Consultant, AFLAC

I have been a member of the Hackensack Regional Chamber for about eight years. I thought it would be a good way to meet other business people in the area, because as you know with Aflac we are a B2B provider of supplemental insurance benefits. I also thought it would be a great way to get involved in the community where I live.

What I Like most about being a member

I think that the people that are part of the Hackensack Chamber are awesome. They're fun, they're great to be around, they are accepting and inviting, they're down to earth, and there are very few people putting on airs.

It's about being around and getting to know people. People started asking questions about different things related to Aflac and there are a few related to health insurance. One of the other members in the Chamber was having some difficulty with her health insurance agent. She had some questions that she was unable to get answered. We sat down and talked about it and I actually was able to work up some quotes for her and helped her modify the insurance plan that she was offering her employees at the time.

That person also became an Aflac customer. She personally purchased an Aflac cancer plan.

The goal was to build the business but also to be involved in the community. Through my involvement in the community I attend the Hackensack Street Fair every year and provide stickers to the children.

I also go to some of the grand openings representing the Chamber as well as help raise funds for different things that we do. This is an opportunity to meet many different people in the community.

How to utilize the Chamber to achieve your goals

The best way to have the Chamber work for you is for you to work for the Chamber. It is not just paying your dues and expecting it all to come to you, but by getting involved. Attending various events whether it's one of the seminars, a breakfast or a dinner, perhaps even a monthly Board meeting, gets you involved. You can also join one of the committees that meet on a regular basis.

I am on a committee and have been almost since I first joined the Chamber. I began as a member at large and have moved up through the ranks to become the chairperson of the Membership Committee.

What being on a committee can do for you

It allows you to **establish closer one-on-one relationships with different people in the Chamber.** As Chairperson of the Membership Committee, part of my job is to be a greeter. I go to all of the events and my goal is to say hello to as many people as I can as they're walking through the door. I introduce those people to others who are good referrals, part of compatible businesses or who could benefit from meeting each other.

You get to help a lot of people and being on the committee also **allows you to really get to know a small group of members on a very intimate basis.** Some of us have developed friendships outside of the Chamber. We go out to dinner, or we go to the theatre together. We've tried to do different things. In the long run **people buy from the people they know, like and trust.** For example, if your role is to market something, then being in the Chamber and **being on a committee enables you to really get to know people and have them get to know you.**

Where to find Meryl: www.aflac.com/meryl_surgan.

CHAPTER Four

Betty Shingelo

Spencer Savings Bank

Spencer Savings Bank encourages its managers to become involved in the local communities in which they do business. I joined the Chamber several years ago to try to expand my relationship with other professionals and to introduce Spencer Savings Bank to other members. I feel that the services that I can provide may help them grow their businesses.

I like meeting new people at the various networking events. I enjoy the informative speakers and the topics they discuss. I feel by **being a member I have an opportunity for me personally and for Spencer Savings Bank to become better known to the membership and to the community.**

Why Join and Participate?

I would recommend the Hackensack Chamber of Commerce to a new member because they are an **active organization and the events are well attended.** The Chamber members are very friendly, outgoing, and always make me feel welcome. I support the efforts of the Chamber and their endeavors.

I attend as many of the events as possible. The one event that I enjoyed was the Moonlight Picnic. It was very well attended. I made many contacts there and also won some prizes from the raffles. This event provided a great deal of exposure to many different professional people, which could turn into business opportunities.

I find that no matter what the events are or how many you attend, it is an opportunity to meet people.

You can find Betty at www.spencersavings.com.

CHAPTER Five

Mike McNamara
General Manager

Maggiano's Little Italy Restaurant

I'm the General Manager of Maggiano's Little Italy Restaurant in Hackensack, New Jersey. I have been a member since day one, which is just over six years when we opened the doors here at our restaurant. We even joined before we opened as a way to spread the word about the restaurant. The Chamber and I have had a great relationship ever since.

The main reason we joined was **marketing: to let the community know that we were here as a resource for a great restaurant,** banquet rooms, delivery, carryout and bar. **We wanted to get the message out to the Hackensack businesses and the Hackensack residents that we want to be an active and positive presence in the community.** It's worked really well.

I would say what I like most about being a member is the **awareness we get in the community. We've hosted several Chamber events here in our beautiful banquet rooms. This helps bring new and old faces** in to let them know that we have banquet rooms and that **we are a pillar in the Hackensack community.**

I think just being able to say that we are a **proud member of the Hackensack Chamber really goes a long way. We have a decal on our front door that says we are a member.** I think it looks good to the community that we've made that commitment to the Chamber.

Chamber can actually help you achieve some of your goals

I would say we've been fortunate to host several Chamber events and I'd like to mention a few that come to mind. We've had many big names here like former Governor Jon Corzine and also Lieutenant Governor Kim Guadagno who have spoken to the Chamber. Those events have **garnered us some good press, local media, and also have resulted in big numbers like 100 plus attendees.** That is definitely something to **expand the brand within Hackensack.**

We have had some of the **Chamber members book banquets with us.** I think that definitely correlates as a return on our investment.

How to have the Chamber help you achieve your goals

I would say that you get out of the Chamber what you put into it. If you're active and involved you're going to get a great deal out of it and you're going to get a nice return on your membership dues. It is something that you've got to work at by keeping in touch with Darlene and with the Chamber. The more involved and engaged you are, the more you're going to get out of that relationship. If you **go to the events where they teach you different things about business or different things about sales and marketing, that's a very tangible reward for your business.**

I'm very happy with the Hackensack Chamber. I think Darlene does a great job running it. We anticipate continuing our membership for many, many years to come.

You can find Mike at www.maggianos.com

CHAPTER Six

Robin C. Ricca

Ricca Auto Body

My name is Robin C. Ricca and I'm a partner with my brother at Ricca Auto Body. I'm a recent member of the Chamber, and that's due to the fact that I was a high school coach for many, many years. Being an ice hockey coach put me in the rink about six nights a week. I also was a baseball coach. Now that I'm older and retired from all coaching, about five years ago, I decided that I had some time available.

I am somewhat partial to children. I found out about the education committee, which is a subcommittee for the Hackensack Regional Chamber of Commerce, and since I have a New Jersey substitute teacher's license, it was a natural fit for me.

What we do is raise enough donations to hold organizational meetings. We have a picnic every year, so on and so forth. We gather money and donations and ads so we are able to offer scholarship money for children from two school systems: **Hackensack High School and the Saddle Brook School System.**

I joined because it was **time for me to give back to my community.** I had been involved in my community for so many years. My children graduated in '97 and I stayed on with the program because I liked it so much I became a paid coach for many years at the high school level.

After retirement, I started to refocus on my business because we had changes going on due to the bad economy. Darlene Damstrom, who's the Executive Director, and I know each other. She's a business client. She said "Well now, you have time to come work on the education committee." I said, "That's not such a bad idea; it's actually a pretty good fit for me. I love kids. I have a sublicense. I've spent, God knows how many years involved with children and coaching and mentoring them."

We also offer mentoring programs through the trade school at our body shop here. We have a program here for the past two years where we take youngsters in from the Bergen County High Schools Technical School. They come in as juniors or seniors and we train them and prepare them for the future as tradesmen. They work one or two days a week, depending on what the program allows.

The Chamber has been wonderful for me in many regards. **Number one: there were many friends there that I had previous established relationships with.** They were clients of mine and I was a client of theirs. **I reconnected with other old friends and more importantly it was an opportunity to** give back to the community. This is my way of saying thank you.

Furthermore I made a tremendous amount of new friends and the circle of friends gets bigger **as we get older. This friend** knows that friend and it turns out to be a wonderful way of networking and accomplishing a number of things all at once.

Why the Chamber had an impact on my business and my life

I'm in my second year as part of the Education Committee. An event that stands out in my mind was the time when the young lady that normally hands out the scholarships at Hackensack High School wasn't able to attend. There were conflicts that night because we had different members from the Education Committee attending different events on the same evening. She asked me if I would do it. I've done a lot of public speaking so that's probably why she chose me. I went over to the high school at 7:00 pm and that was a very, very pleasant experience, because, like I said, I'm partial to children. I had no idea how nice Hackensack High School was, because I had not coached there.

Although I knew the Hackensack ice hockey coach from my years of coaching, I only participated in the schools such as, Indian Hills, Ramapo and River Dell Regional High School. What I realized is that there were so many people that I knew: Deputy Mayors and many customers whose cars we serviced. I went into this forum with literally hundreds of people for a wonderful evening where they handed out so many scholarships.

The kids were doing well in school. I now look at the school system in a completely different way because it has a staff of wonderful young administrators and the kids are really appreciative. Some of them are from families that needed some financial assistance. Some of them were from families that had kids with high grades. **It was nice to see dozens and dozens of scholarships being given out to the kids that represent the future of our community.**

Real benefits you get by utilizing the Chamber:

I find that when you join an organization that is giving back to the community, you're going to encounter the nicer business people. You're going to get those that run a clean ship, and develop an ethical business. They do things the correct way: One gets two and two gets four.

What happens is, **not only do the children benefit because of the networking, the businesses benefits.** I have new clients here as a result of my efforts of giving back. All of that is because you **go out** to network at one of these events where we have Texas Hold'Em or we have a fundraiser or picnic **and you just shake hands.**

For me, all the people that I have met in the Chamber haven't incurred any problems in their businesses. I've only met people that pay their bills on time, run their businesses to the best of their ability, are education and continuing education oriented, and like to give back to the community. Hackensack's been very good to me so why wouldn't I want to give back? This is what I say to the ones that aren't members.

"I feel an obligation to give back as a businessman to the community that my business and my employees benefit from."

I became involved with the Education Committee because of former Chamber President Donald Perlman who works a couple of doors away from me. He's quite a passive personality and I'm a very aggressive personality. Donald and I work very well together. It's a good marriage. He works for me and I work for him.

We fix his cars, he does my letters.

He's the one that introduced me to Darlene. It turns out that Darlene's husband and I went to high school together!

You can find Robin at www.riccaautobody.com.

CHAPTER Seven

Anthony Ursillo

Hackensack Regional Chamber of Commerce President 2013-2015

Commercial Real Estate Broker

I have been a member of the Hackensack Regional Chamber for 10 years now. When I came onboard it was quite different than it is today. There was far less membership but I felt it could be a place where I could grow and hopefully let my influence bring other businesses to join. There were very few members and it wasn't really up to par. I was hoping to contribute and make things better and therefore, it would grow.

I truly enjoy the membership, the Board of Directors and the past Presidents and Vice Presidents. You make a lot of friends. It doesn't take very long and that is the part about it that I like best.

I've been fortunate with regard to the actual business. **My business has been affected by membership** and I've enjoyed some new business relationships. I've done fairly well with them. It's been a very good membership for me. I then got involved with the Board of Directors and that helped even more.

One of the things that I became involved with was the Events Committee and I Co-Chaired that with Diane Some. We worked very hard on changing and growing the Chamber. Just to give you an idea on the growth, we have a yearly gala and when we took over, there were only 60, 70, 80 people attending. **Last year we had over 300 attendees.** It grew tremendously. We achieved that in about four years. It's not just me, it's a team effort and we were very successful at working and achieving new goals, new memberships..

Linda Sylvestri, Darlene Damstrom and I worked very hard. We're very proud of that.

Why Join and Participate?

I would suggest and encourage more participation. You should be involved as much as possible. Network as much as you can within the body of the membership as well as the offices. Get to know as many people as you can. Make friends, which is easy. Enjoy good fellowship as well as business, because if you just join and stand still nothing's going to happen.

Some people think: *I'm a member of the Chamber of Commerce and I don't see an increase in business. Although I haven't done anything and I haven't gone to any meetings, and I haven't gone to any of the events, I expected that they were going to deliver it to me.* That's not the way it is. You need to take the time and make an effort to get involved, and meet new people, and discuss with them commonalities. You should be **telling them what your business is about and what your goals are and what you'd like to achieve.**

Our membership is strong now and it's been growing. **I would suggest going to every single event that you can and attend the meetings.** I think it'll do wonders. Nothing's going to happen for you, you have to make it happen.

I would encourage members to make themselves known to as many people as possible. I know we, the Board of Directors, have been thinking about accelerating our interaction with not only the existing membership, but new members coming in. Without participation and without knowing who the members, officers and the directors are, you are going to stay at a flat level. **You have to get in there and participate and network.**

Let people know who you are and then also learn who they are because that could affect tomorrow's business for you. If you just don't do anything and just say, *"Oh I'm a member of the Chamber,"* forget about being successful, because, just like with anything else, what you put in is what you're going to get out of it.

CHAPTER Eight

Stacey Reich-Benjamin

At Home Companions

My name is Stacey Reich-Benjamin and my company is At Home Companions. I have been a member of the Hackensack Chamber almost nine years.

I would say that the most positive experience about being part of the Chamber would be **meeting other people in and out of the business community.** Because I live in Hackensack, I also meet **people who are running the community.** I enjoy **having an opportunity to get to know those people and be part of organizations.**

I'm the chairwoman of the Education Committee. We hold a fundraiser every year. I would say that's probably when I get the most from the Chamber.

Quite honestly, the reason that I was introduced to the Chamber is because when I started my company, I was working with a volunteer from an organization called SCORE. I worked with a SCORE mentor for almost three years. We used to meet in Darlene's office. I became very familiar and friendly with Darlene and the Chamber. I think that joining was the natural thing to do. Originally I joined looking for business. I don't know how much business I've gotten from the Chamber, but I feel like **I have certainly established relationships in the community because of the it.**

This has been invaluable to me. I know that's not what people want to hear but it's the truth.

Why Join and Participate?

I think joining the Chamber, depending on the kind of business you have, means that there certainly is potential to **create business relationships and to acquire business. Joining also establishes a sense of integrity inside the community. If you are part of community organizations and are known throughout those organizations, I think that will naturally promote business.**

This **gives you a sense of being established.** If you go to an event and people recognize you (people such as the mayor), I think that that automatically gives your business a little more value.

CHAPTER Nine

Wendy Richmond

Memorable Marketing System

I first came upon the Hackensack Regional Chamber of Commerce when I was participating in a Multi-Chamber Networking Event. I walked up to Darlene Damstrom, who is the Executive Director of the Chamber, and purchased my ticket for the event. We chatted for just a few moments and I gave her one of my business cards.

A couple of weeks after the event, I got an e-mail from Meryl Surgan, asking me if I was available to speak to their members at one of their upcoming Chamber Breakfasts. Since speaking is one of the ways I help small business owners as well as promote my own business, I said, "Yes!"

Within a month's time, I was THE speaker for the semi-annual membership event and I spoke about **Five Memorable Marketing Strategies to Grow Your Business at Lightning Speed.** The event was a big hit! There were at least 45 people in attendance and my presentation was well received.

In addition to introducing myself to a great group of people, **I landed new business immediately from my talk.** This all happened before I was even a member! Once I was working with a few of the members and helping them with their businesses, I thought I would really like to join and see what else I could do to help the membership.

I have served as Chairperson for the Marketing Committee and facilitator for the writing and printing of this book, as well as using my marketing expertise to help the Chamber with its educational programming and events. This has definitely elevated my visibility in the community and among the membership.

As has been said earlier in this book, getting known and being seen is one of THE biggest keys to success at the Chamber. My whole reason for joining was to be part of a community, be seen by many people who share the same types of values, easily get known in this community, give back to this community and grow my business through this community.

I have heard many successful Chamber Members say that **you get out what you put into it.** Now, I firmly believe this to be the case. **The more I do for the Chamber, the more I get known and ultimately, the more business I get.** Plus, I do like the other benefits **of being part of a nice community and giving back to help the young people of the Hackensack, New Jersey area.**

You can find Wendy Richmond at
www.memorablemarketingsystem.com

CHAPTER Ten

18 Success Strategies for Hackensack Regional Chamber of Commerce Members

Here is a list of 18 ways you can utilize being a member of the Hackensack Regional Chamber of Commerce. Use it as a check list to see how many you are currently using and how many more you could implement.

1. **Go to events and meet people.** The more people you meet, the more you will have an opportunity to garner more business, either through your direct contact or as a referral. Plus, you will be able to refer others, which makes you a great "go to" person for those who need help. Not a bad way to be seen!

2. **Offer the members something special as a way to introduce your business.** If you are a restaurant owner, offer a free dessert with a meal. If you are a retailer, issue a coupon. If you are a service provider, present a special deal and/or some kind of information other than your brochure. *(Everyone gives a brochure. Do something to make your business stand out!)*

3. **Get to know who is part of the Chamber,** so you can be a referral source. The more you refer, the more you are referred. It is the law of reciprocity.

4. **Join a committee:** We know your time is limited. Because you don't have lots of time to give, you need to invest it for the best ROI (Return on Investment). Being on a committee gives you the biggest ROI, because you get to intimately know other committee members faster. You are seen as a giver. Plus, you get the opportunity to introduce yourself as a committee member, instead of just a businessperson wanting business.

5. **Send something of interest in the mail to the Members.** I am sure you understand that most people won't do business with you just because you are a Chamber member. They need to get to know you and your business first. When you communicate with the Membership in a way that is helpful, you are seen as a different kind of business. It shows you care about the members. Once you are seen in this light, you will find more opportunities coming to you.

6. **Recommend others to join the Chamber:** When you do this, you are seen as an asset to the Chamber and what goes around definitely comes around.

7. **Get to know the Executive Director, Darlene Damstrom:** When you get to know Darlene, as she wrote before in this book, she can recommend you. She knows everyone and people do go to her for recommendations.

8. **Go to the educational seminars, Webinars, meetings, etc.:** The Chamber is there to help your business in any way it can. One big advantage is getting learning opportunities at a reduced fee. If you just participated, learned something, applied it to your business, and got business because of it, just think what your ROI is for just that one event!

9. **Find complimentary Chamber members businesses to do referral partnerships.** Instead of just looking for direct business from the members, find complimentary businesses who have the same ideal customers/clients and set up a referral partnership. You could do this with several different members. Because you are a member, just like them, you could use that to your advantage in partnering with them.

10. **Put together your own events and invite the Chamber members to attend.** No one said that you had to have every event done through the Chamber itself. You could easily put together your own seminar, workshop, cocktail hour, etc. Invite the members and see who comes. The ones who attend will be valuable people to offer your product/service to and/or partner with and/or give referrals to, etc.

11. **Put together partnership events:** You can find your complimentary Chamber businesses and put on an event together. If you both use your own lists, plus, invite Chamber Members, you can create something quite memorable and valuable. If it works well, you can do it over and over again.

12. **Send out a Direct Mail Piece to those members who would be ideal clients/customers for your business:** Chances are not everyone in the Chamber is a good fit for your business. You can look yourself or ask Darlene Damstrom, Executive Director, who would be a good fit and specifically target those members to offer your products/services.

13. **Put together an Education Teleseminar:** Invite the members for an educational teleseminar. This way you don't have to spend tons of money on a space. Again, those who attend would be very good people to get to know and of course, offer your services.

14. **Stay "Top of Mind" in the Membership:** The members cannot refer you if they don't know who you are and what your company does. You can attend the events, send monthly physical newsletters, ask members if they would like to opt in to your e-mail list, etc. If you are top of mind, you can more easily be referred and/or get new business because the membership knows about you.

15. **Offer to do a Free Seminar through the Chamber:** Instead of, or as well as, doing a seminar on your own, you can offer to give a free seminar during one of the monthly breakfast meetings and/or other times during the year and have the Chamber promote it. You never know unless you ask!

16. **Use the fact that you are "A Proud Member of the Hackensack Regional Chamber of Commerce" as part of your marketing.** People respect the Chamber and

what it stands for, so being attached to this group shows you are part of the community. Plus, the Chamber does many charity events. You can also participate in those charity events and use that in your marketing. Again, it makes you look like a stand up business who cares about the community.

17. **Host an Event at Your Place of Business:** When you are the host, members come out and get to see what you do first hand. It goes a long way towards getting the members to know, like and trust you and ultimately, your business.

18. **Speak Up! Let the Committees Know What You Want from Your Membership:** No one can read your mind. If there is something you want or need to help you with your business, you need to tell someone. If you have suggestions for things, events, etc. the best way to make those happen is to tell someone and help make it happen.

We try to add things for our members based on what we hear they need, so why not have what you want or need get put into the mix. If it is possible to do, we will help to make it happen.

CHAPTER Eleven

Success Strategies for Potential

Hackensack Regional Chamber of Commerce Members

Don't Just Jump In

Be Strategic!!

For anyone thinking about joining the Hackensack Regional Chamber of Commerce, there are a few things to **think about before you join.**

1. Based on the previous chapter, ask yourself, "Will any of these strategies work for my business?" If so, then joining the Chamber is a good idea.

2. Have a real plan in place to help you hit the ground running for success.

3. Talk with Darlene Damstrom, Executive Director, about your business and the possibilities for it being a good fit.

4. Talk with other successful Chamber members to see that joining the Chamber can be a great boost for your business.

5. Attend one event first to get a feel for the group. Is it somewhere you feel comfortable? Do they have good events? Can you see yourself belonging and participating in this group?

6. Find out how many members are in this group and know that there is a targeted group of people that you can offer your product/services to who belong, "just like you" to the same group.

Once you do these things, you will have much more knowledge about the kinds of successes you could have being a part of our Chamber. Plus, with this book, you now have many ideas for **How to Make Your Hackensack Regional Chamber of Commerce Membership Give You the Most Return on Your Investment!**

CHAPTER Twelve

5 Insider Successful Networking Strategies

Every successful Chamber member knows that networking is one of THE best ways to grow their business. A lot has been written about networking, so we wanted to give you some insider success strategies that you may not find in any other book.

Here are the 5 Insider Successful Networking Strategies:

1. **Know who your Ideal Client/Customer is before you go to an event.** If you know who your ideal clients/customers are before you go to an event, you will be more focused on who you should talk to first.

   Here is an example. If you sell financial services and you know that your best client/customer is a man who is between 50-70, scan the room for men that look like your ideal client/customer and make sure to talk to them first.

This will save you time in the long run. If you spend time talking to just anybody, chances are you will not find your networking experience as profitable as it could be. We hear complaints about not getting business from the membership and this is one of the biggest reasons why.

2. **Speak with Darlene Damstrom, Executive Director, about who in the Chamber would be a good match for your business.** Darlene has been with the Chamber for 13 years and knows the members really well. If she gets to know you and your business, she can help you be successful by introducing you to more of the right kinds of members.

3. **Have conversations that are not just about What you do for a living.** One of the biggest challenges is to go to networking events with the attitude that I am going to make connections to start a relationship. As you have read, more than once in this book, it really is about relationships. Most people don't meet someone once and do business with them. (Unless they are in immediate need of your service and they know, like and trust you.) They need to get to know you, make sure you really know what you are talking about and can really help them or someone they know.

Make it a goal to go to the networking events to get to know the members as people first, without any selling. You will be amazed what could happen!

4. **Set a goal to talk with at least three people.** Successful networkers set goals of what they want to accomplish at

the networking event before they attend. This is crucial and empowering. So many people go to these events and just kind of wander around hoping to talk with someone. Or they spend all of their time talking to just one person. If you set a goal to talk with at least three people, you have a better chance of finding someone who would be interested in your product/service.

5. **The key to successful networking is FOLLOW UP.** You spend time and money to go to an event, meet people, have conversations with them and leave. Now is the most important part, **FOLLOW UP.** One of the best things you can do after you meet someone who is a good prospect for your product/service is to invite them for coffee or lunch. Get to know them. Have them get to know you. Once they know, like and trust you, chances are good they will do business with you or at least refer you to someone they know who could be a good fit for your business.

If you can't go for coffee or lunch, then start sending them information about your business. Don't just send a brochure. That is what everyone else does. Be different, stand out. Offer them a discount or free trial, something like that.

Just like they say in the lottery commercial, "You can't win, if you don't play." The same thing is true of networking. You can't win at networking, unless you are out there networking and doing it strategically.

Final Thoughts

You Get What You Put In

Thank you for reading this book. We do hope that it has been helpful in showing you that there are many ways to utilize the Chamber. We are here to help in any way we can.

As many of our successful members say, "You get what you put in." We are here to help those who ultimately help themselves.

We look forward to working with you as a current member or a potential member, to get everything you want from your membership and much, much more!!

Sincerely,

The Hackensack Regional Chamber of Commerce

Now check out our very **Special Offer** for Hackensack Regional Chamber of Commerce book readers who want to become new members! ⟶

Special Offer for Hackensack Regional Chamber of Commerce Book Readers Who Want to Become New Members

As a "thank you" for taking the time to read our book, we want to give you something special for becoming a new member. In addition to all of the wonderful business building resources that you have access to over the next year, we would like to give you "3 Additional Months of Your Membership." That's 15 months for your 12 month investment, when you join!

All you have to do is <u>call</u> our Chamber office at **(201) 489-3700** or <u>e-mail</u> us at **membership@hackensackchamber.org**. Tell us you read our book and would like to join our Chamber Membership. That's it! That's all you have to do.

We look forward to helping you grow your business!

Hackensack Regional Chamber of Commerce Membership Committee

Strategic Notes

Strategic Notes

Strategic Notes

Strategic Notes

Strategic Notes